Bhutan BETWEEN HEAVEN AND EARTH

Bhutan

between

HEAVEN & EARTH

PHOTOGRAPHS BY MARY PECK   ESSAY BY KARMA URA

MERLIN PRESS, SANTA FE   PHOENIX ART MUSEUM

Karma Ura

TRADITION AND CULTURE IN BHUTAN

1. THE COUNTRY

Despite its small size, Bhutan is actually a large country as defined by cultural, ethnic, and biological diversity. Although the country measures only forty-six thousand square kilometers in area, the land is not flat, and micro-climates abound. Entering the next valley, things look slightly different; a little further still and the framework of the previous landscape does not apply.

The contour of the landscape has guided the settlement of this country in important ways. Sacred, divine, or auspicious forms are ascribed to the features of the land—a *dzong* may be established on the nose of an elephant; a temple, on the back of a moving tortoise. If the land looks like a moving snake, the head of the snake will be pinned down with a chorten or temple to tame that place.

This mythology can carry ancient wisdom. For example, at the southern approach road to my own village, there is a narrow river gorge. In that gorge, according to myth, once lay the palace of Tinleytagsey, the guardian deity of Ura. He is still worshipped as the one who controls the weather and protects us in all our daily tasks. A forest of ancient spruce ran along the river. We believed that if we picked firewood from that place, bad weather—early frost, heavy rains, hailstorms—would follow, so the grove was well protected. When DANTAK, the Indian road construction company, opened the modern road, they decimated that forest. Young spruce are coming up again, but it doesn't look dark and mysterious like it did during my childhood.

In losing that forest, we discovered one of its important functions: it provided a very good windscreen from the cold air on the southern side of the village, and it played a role in lowering the temperature for the crops in the valley. Without any scientific inquiry, we have no proof of this, but I can easily imagine that all deity worship based in the topography of the landscape has corresponding ecological benefits.

Traditionally, Bhutanese live close to nature. This means that the food chain is more or less completed within one's own valley. The people live embedded in the production processes of their own specific regions, where they live most of their lives. They thus develop a deep and strong knowledge over the generations of what that land can and cannot support. When that knowledge is ingrained in the lifestyle, the relationship between man and nature is very stable over the centuries, because the rules are known. The communities endure; they don't flourish and die in a continuous cycle.

For many communities in Bhutan, the living standard is supportable over a long period of time.

Bhutan is a Buddhist country, and Buddhism greatly informs our culture. The principle of coexistence found in Buddhism—the right of all sentient beings to live—is manifested in our institutions and rules, at least those unwritten rules and regulations that influence the access of individuals to resources such as water, forests, fuel, grass, temples, or any kind of space, be it social, political, economic, or environmental in nature. Many different rules are followed by members of the community, who become members only by virtue of following these ways. The rules are unwritten but they are there, and they are very important for maintaining tradition.

Of course, Bhutan has many institutions that regulate all sorts of relations in addition to those between man and natural resources; others include the relationship between humans and deities, or between individual villagers and the district administration. For example, an individual has obligations to the monasteries and monks, and likewise the monks are concerned about their communities. The task of reinforcing culture and tradition is really a permanent one, and should be integrated into planning. But ethnographers have not produced enough tools for studying this, and the economists who have developed such tools talk only about economic growth, and not about the value of culture and tradition.

2. THE PHILOSOPHY

Some very farsighted people within the Bhutanese government have advocated a degree of caution in rapid modernization, accepting as axiomatic the importance of preserving culture and tradition. The government of Bhutan, at least on a theoretical level, has always promoted five very important principles of development. The first is the development of economic self-reliance, meaning that ultimately we are not dependent on aid; we should be able to finance development out of our own revenue, which grows by developing our own resources. Preservation of the environment is the second principle of development; decentralization of economic planning is the third, and preservation of culture and tradition is the fourth. The fifth principle is the policy of equal development across regions, meaning that the same standard of living must be available for every Bhutanese.

The term Gross National Happiness (GNH) denotes Bhutan's attempt to create a society in which collective happiness is the goal of governance. For this, we must pay tribute to His Majesty the Fourth King of Bhutan, the true author of GNH. In 1972, when His Majesty was still a teenage monarch, he spoke to an American newspaper about GNH, and questioned the prevailing assumption that GDP alone was a reasonable measure of happiness and wellbeing in society. This question was breathtakingly bold and profound, all the more so because it came from the mind of a teenager.

GNH should not be misunderstood as a kind of simple, reductionist framework in which citizens are only concerned with happiness for themselves, obsessed with pleasurable feelings. Rather, GNH is a very rich development philosophy, and also an enlightened personal ethos. Criticism that Bhutan attempts only to maximize subjective happiness is quite misplaced. For example, if we consider ourselves only as pleasure-maximizing beings, and are not concerned with justice and compassion, we could just take drugs and be happy. But there is no humanity in that approach.

GNH really stands for a holistic vision guiding governance and development; it also stands for the holistic needs of the people. At one level, GNH addresses material needs in the physical realm; at another, it addresses the inner realm—the intangible—as wellbeing also accrues from the immaterial. Furthermore, GNH signifies the preservation and renewal of a range of wealth or capital. When we talk about "wealth," we normally mean only material things, so the word "capital" may be more accurate. Material wealth or capital is measured well by GDP, but other types of capital also should be valued and measured: ecological capital; social capital, things like trust, reciprocity, and positive emotions; human-resource capital; and cultural and spiritual capital. If we value and measure the ups and downs of all of these types of capital over time, we get a true picture of whether society is developing or regressing. If we just focus on measures of economic capital and ignore what is happening to other forms of capital, we will likely find ourselves one day facing great costs, our lives quite impoverished.

For this reason, with GNH we take into account a wider set of resources, and point out that these must be preserved if we are to continue pursuing collective happiness in a holistic way. This was the essence of the message His Majesty the Fourth King communicated when he said, "GNH is more important than GDP." During his reign, the actual road map of laws and policies for good development was developed, a legacy that we enjoy today. The Fourth King firmly believed that happiness is an indicator, a signifier and a sign, of good development and good society. He also believed in the legitimacy of public deliberation, public discussion, and public opinion in defining any goal. His visions of GNH and of democracy for our country are complementary. We must strive to be loyal to both: through democracy—through enlightened citizenship and enlightened views of citizenship—we will come to prefer collective happiness as the goal of society.

Different groups have different interpretations of GNH. Is there a way we can agree on some acceptable definition? Actually, when we measure levels of subjective happiness, there is no need for individual happiness to hold the same meaning for everyone. What makes an individual happy at any particular moment is entirely up to that person, without need for further verification. The goal of GNH in terms of governance, however, is collective happiness, as opposed to individualistic or private happiness. The means of obtaining happiness will certainly differ according to age, taste, and personal capacity. But from a GNH point of view, the most important thing is that the individual should not achieve happiness without regard for the cost to society—either to humans or to other beings. If one's happiness is achieved by passing negative consequences on to others, collective happiness is not possible. In order to achieve our collective happiness, we must elevate our vision beyond the maximization of irresponsible and egocentric happiness, and limit the negative consequences of obtaining our own happiness.

Some doubt also remains as to whether individual choice can always, unmistakably, lead to individual happiness. We know very well that we can choose the wrong options; our judgment and choices are not always correct. From a Buddhist point of view, we as people are prone to illusory beliefs, leading us to behaviors and choices that cause the course of our lives to deviate from happiness; the teachings enjoin us constantly to be aware of that fact. We come back to the realization that, although individuals may strive for happiness by their own efforts, if the government does not create macroconditions and policies that cultivate happiness, the individual's chances of succeeding will be lower and narrower. Take, for example, the domains of environment, community relationships, good governance, health, and education, all of which are very important to our satisfaction and happiness. These things are influenced by public policy; if public policy is wrong, our chances of realizing wellbeing or happiness are greatly decreased.

The discourse conducted by television, radio, and newspapers is vital in stimulating and deepening a popular conceptualization of GNH outside academic research groups. The public must understand GNH and contribute to its formulation; the media has played a vital role in this. GNH itself has appealed to national and international journalists, perhaps due to the inherent power in the idea. Part of the international coverage of GNH is stimulated by a shared curiosity: What is this country doing? In more serious terms, the international interest also reflects a deep-seated longing for genuine, alternative, holistic development.

We may ask whether all of this chatter and conversation on GNH is true to the original intention and proposition of His Majesty the Fourth King. Let's go back to that time. The experience of development worldwide since 1972 shows the King's proposition to be absolutely pertinent, because much of economic development has failed, somehow, to provide satisfaction, especially in the industrialized, wealthy North, where the level of satisfaction is stagnating even though economic prosperity is rising. As so often happens with born leaders, the Fourth King's insights were ahead of their time by decades.

Of course, a society is not created in a single moment by a god or some such circumstance. What GNH means is that a society adjusts and adapts increasingly towards certain goals that it defines for itself—in this case, collective happiness. In part, such adaptations are continuations of efforts in Bhutan's past; in documents dating as far back as 1729, happiness is mentioned explicitly as the purpose of governance. The present experiment taking place in Bhutan was initiated and guided by the enlightened leadership of the Fourth King, and is now continued and developed by the Fifth King. Competing and conflicting interests and challenges may take us in a different direction. But if we are very conscious of the goals and pitfalls and wish to pursue this course, we can design a society based on collective happiness.

I think conveying the idea of GNH to laypeople and to the younger generation will involve quite different content and methods. Youth, for example, are full of hope and idealism; they may be largely fulfilled because of the highly progressive nature of society. But as it is with life, a good proportion of them will also find that their aspirations can't be met—they will have to reconcile their expectations to something else. Most of these young people—ninety-two percent or so, thanks to the massive education movement of our government—are enrolled in our schools. The education sector is confronted with the choice of emphasizing literacy, employment skills, or values. Whatever emphasis educators choose, young people need a framework for understanding life as a whole, so that the disruptive and dislocating experience of adolescence can be subsumed within a larger context. I think that this framework can be supported by a simplified version of GNH focused on emotional balance and psychological wellbeing. For youth as a whole, I would suggest a greater understanding of emotions and values; finding balance between negative and positive emotions is critical.

For laypeople, who are mostly village-farmers and householders, I would suggest community relationships as an area for particular attention. The bonds between the members of a community feed and thrive on trust, volunteerism, reciprocity, and cooperation, because community members are bounded geographically and socially, and have to work out a way of living harmoniously. Conflicts and litigations, divorces and factionalism signal the breakdown of this social bond and the collapse of peace and harmony in the community. Underlying all of this is the breakdown of relationships. In the end, a community is sustained by good, positive relationships among its members, which give rise spontaneously to happiness. Relationships are fundamental to happiness; we can have better relations, not necessarily when we have more money, more goods, or better houses, but especially when we have better motivations and intentions—these heal us.

If we cannot maintain healthy relationships in family and community, this will translate into costs to the judiciary and law-enforcement agencies, for whose services we pay through taxes and other revenues. In themselves, good relationships, community vitality, a sense of trust, reciprocity, and volunteerism are important to happiness. If these break down, the other resources of the country are also sapped. More money must be invested in the judiciary to solve divorces and litigate conflicts; more money must be spent on policing and security apparatuses. It is wrong to focus on objective conditions as yielding happiness, which is really a by-product of improving relationships. Therefore, we can understand holistic development ultimately as improvement in the relational capacity of people.

At this time, we must understand that development is a non-linear process—things can backfire. The situation is changing; the pace is rapid and the side effects are becoming more noticeable in social, cultural, and ecological terms. As for the latter, we already notice pollution in the air and on the horizon. In social terms, migration is posing problems: congestion and urban lifestyles on the one hand, and on the other, empty villages and older people on their own. Equally on the cultural side, challenges to Bhutanese values and institutions are apparent. One intention of GNH is to prevent these costs right at the commencement of development.

3. ENCOUNTER WITH THE WEST

Change is coming faster now, due to a widening sphere of contact enabled by the introduction of more modern communications systems, including the Internet and cable television. Better surface and air transport has increased the volume of tourism traffic. All of these changes are really part of the opening up that has been underway in Bhutan since 1961, but this movement is now a bit more indiscriminate because of the somewhat doctrinaire acceptance of globalization and free trade. Once these forces are accepted, it is difficult to control the pace of change. This is the period we have entered now; the rate of change is bound to increase.

Bhutanese don't think in terms of the national/international dichotomy at all, but only in terms of the past and present. The past was acceptable in many ways, except for the lack of material affluence. People believe that the past was good, and that the best features of the past should continue. Security existed at a national level and in community life, and family relations were strong. There must be continuity with the past because there were many good things in the past, but there are also things that should be discarded. I must confess, however, that we are not very capable of selecting what is good from outside and inside, because we don't understand what is outside. We are in the paradoxical situation of accepting more and more from outside, even though we really don't know the world beyond Bhutan. The popular image is drawn from television, an image of the West in which all are beautiful, all are good, all are happy, and all are clean, neat, and strong. To make a judgment about what to bring in from outside, we must understand the cultural and political context that gave rise to these things.

In modernization, no clear process whereby we learn from the lessons of others really exists. Learning from others' mistakes is more easily said than done. Long-term impacts are not analyzed; instead, we believe that some nations are very successful at this moment in time, and therefore what they do must be right. And government agencies themselves campaign for certain ways of doing things. Projects advocated by international aid agencies serve in part as vehicles for transmitting these campaigns.

With urbanization—one aspect of modernization—the coherence of village life is disturbed; people don't develop the same knowledge. To begin with, people today don't have as diverse a lifestyle as their forebears. In the village, for example, a farmer is not only a farmer, but also a carpenter, a painter, and a dancer, as well as a part-time trapper, wood collector, and house builder—his skill range is very wide. A farmer is also a part-time animal husbandry man, and so he knows about breeds and animals' habits. A deity worshipper, he knows a little bit about the polytheistic structure of belief. A farmer continually harvests, observing the lifecycles of trees and plants, thus developing an interesting insight into nature. The exercise of his interest and expression of his potential are very high, because over the course of the year, he does so many different activities.

With increased development, people become mono-functional. They study to become economists or typists. Their "knowledge" is much narrower than their parents' knowledge. Talented people may be living in a valley, but because of this narrowing of skills, they have no relationship with the environment around them; this is an even bigger problem on a national scale. The food chain of the huge urban area of Thimphu is connected to India through imports. People don't do anything with their own land, or understand anything about the ecology of their area. They breathe the air and drink the water, but they don't understand the deep processes involved in the most important things that give them life. This sort of disjunction develops in an urban area such as Thimphu, and it is crucial that people fight it and reconnect to the environment.

For Bhutan, preservation of culture and tradition presents a major challenge, especially because we don't have our own huge center of gravity, something that countries sometimes achieve by force of ideology, by size, or by their innate strengths. All that Bhutan has is a very long history of isolation. If we imitate other countries, shifting more and more to an externally based perspective, we will lose our sense of cohesion around a self-referential point of view—a Bhutanese "way" in terms of philosophy, political principles, organizational ideas, educational systems, and resource-management knowledge. Can values that emphasize decentralization and utilize local perspectives become a coherent set of elements that enable us to preserve and sustain our culture?

Historically, the local ecology—the forest, the wildlife, the rivers—was always in the custody of the local inhabitants. During this recent phase of rapid infusion of ideas from abroad, people have learned the idea that a central agency is needed to enforce environmental regulations in order to best protect the environment. But the environment is everywhere, and it can't be protected in this manner. At the end of the day, our decisions must take into consideration the ecology of the areas affected by those decisions, and people who live far away from those areas have no clue. To preserve the environment, people must know the environment. Locals may not have written books about it, but they know the ecology where they live. This is more important than the wider democratic or economic context, especially if the community is not integrated with the rest of the country, the region, or the world in terms of economy and politics. It is really the ecological specificity of our decisions that makes them successful or not, so we must decentralize everything from industries to administration.

A recent decentralization act put in writing what the people were already doing. The protection of rivers, streams, and lakes; the safe disposal of waste bottles; the choice of programs; the access to cable TV; and the posting of billboards on the highways—these and other decisions are completely up to each community. Regulation that is very decentralized is allowed in our country, and it has already had some practical effect. Many places started banning the use of plastic bags before the central government took any action. Districts began to declare small pieces of legislation—such as not allowing alcohol to be consumed in a given area on a commercial scale. Imagine the implications of this. Suppose, for example, that a district is allowed to choose the cable channels that it receives. This may seem like a minor decision, but actually it is a major decision affecting our lives, because what TV channels we see and what sort of information is available to us changes the fabric of our thinking.

Decentralization, therefore, is already going on. The guardianship of the environment is reverting to the villages once again. They are authorized to establish parks, scenic spots, and what we call in Bhutan the "palaces of the deities." Mountains, forests, sacred groves, and deep pools in the rivers are very often viewed as abodes of a deity, and now locals can designate a place as such an abode. Locals are allowed to have a say on the alignment of the highways, and on the forest-management plan. The forest department may develop a management plan that includes the extraction of timber from a certain area where it would be profitable, but the local community has a say in that.

Of course, these new rules are neither exploited nor understood fully, but the legal context thus created is very favorable to decision-making by communities, and some communities are taking up these opportunities. For example, the district just outside the boundary of Thimphu has a mountain behind it. The community leader there found that most of the residents of Thimphu wished to have timber and fuel drawn from the forest on the mountain. The city's population is huge compared to the size of the forest. The community leader saw that such a practice could be detrimental to the life of the community over the long term, and he expressed formally that his district was not in favor of any further management plan being implemented there. In this way, the custody of natural resources can revert to the local communities.

In my opinion, infrastructures that actually support decentralization are electricity and roads. I like rural settlement and the lifestyle that goes with it, and if these two infrastructures are not established, people will move to urban areas. In certain places, motor roads may have actually served to draw people to urban areas, but this is not the case here. When roads are constructed, people stay. The consequences of not constructing roads seem to be more hazardous socially and economically in the long run. Roads relieve the burden of having to transport things slowly on human backs. From the environmental and geotechnical points of view, road building is challenging. Parts of the country are extremely rugged and steep, and there is the danger that if roads are not constructed properly, instability in the land surface may result.

Ultimately, however, roads define access. If we do not construct roads to valleys and mountains where the population is scattered, migration from these places to urban areas will inevitably take place much faster, and these remote settlements will gradually die. We will end up with the majority of the Bhutanese people congregated in one metropolis. That, I feel, is not good for any aspect of Bhutan—for the happiness of the individuals or for the rural-based culture of this country. The urbanization process has unfavorable consequences for both ecology and lifestyle; far better, in my opinion, to live in the tranquil, natural environment of rural areas. Real communities can exist only in rural areas constituted by a few hundred individuals who grow up together and live together well, and who have many shared and common interests. Urban life is a bit different; it doesn't seem to foster such things. On these grounds, therefore, I support rural access very much.

Incidentally, aid donors are not interested in preserving culture; development and aid policies are designed for different purposes—to alleviate poverty, gender inequality, and environmental degradation. These are not vital issues in this country, as we have taken care of them already. With a strong base in these areas, we are very close to delivering ourselves from the want of any material needs. Per capita income is inherently defective in measuring the living standard of a country that is not monetized, and that depends so much on natural resources that do not pass through a market. I am always dissatisfied with household income and expenditure surveys, which fail to capture many things that promote our wellbeing. We have no hunger, no destitution, and no homelessness. We do want to bring people to a comfortable standard of living. Nobody should waste his days and energies just to fill up his belly; that's not the idea of this country, nor of our king. It is taken for granted that everybody must have this standard. But we must not cross a threshold of illusion, where we believe that more and more money will actually bring us peace and better wellbeing. It is a much bigger task for the whole population to build a shared belief, a shared understanding that we may not become happier by fulfilling more desires and acquiring more things that we mistakenly believe will make us happy. To lift people up to a very comfortable life and then convince them that this is where they should stay to be happy is much more difficult.

Leadership and literacy need to be distinguished. We have very good leaders who are not literate. What they have is integrity, wisdom, and foresight; they don't need accounting skills, or the ability to write up minutes. I don't see lack of literacy as a crucial shortcoming at this stage. Of course, if all of society is literate and the means of all communication is writing, then literacy is essential. But right now, Bhutan has an orally based culture that has evolved enough not to be dwarfed or overshadowed or completely disadvantaged by the lack of writing. People who are good leaders have good motives—some selflessness and energy to put into common interests. They don't use systematic decision-making tools like cost-benefit analysis, but they have an intuitive ability to make the right choices and to appeal to everybody to accept them. Thus our community leaders may not be qualified in the sense of literacy, but the decisions they make are not necessarily inferior to those made by postgraduates. In fact, when postgraduates try to make decisions, the result is always expensive; that's true with bureaucracy as a whole.

We must believe that every place under the sun has potential. This is different from the Western-based idea of individuality. In Buddhist culture, each of us is supposed to be an incipient Buddha; we all have the potential to be Buddha. As every individual has potential, so does the land where we live; each community will have some potential. We should investigate what particular tools and opportunities can be used to realize that potential. In the past, the people of Bhutan directed their study towards understanding the mind itself. The Buddhist specialty is always probing such questions as, "Why do I think like this? Where does my desire come from? Where does it go?" The modern world needs to be concerned with these questions, but they have not yet entered the modern educational system. In this sociologically interesting period in which we live, we await the outcome of our current choices and look to see what the world will become.

{ Plates }

15

Old Man at Leisure

Sacred or secular
   manners and conventions
      make no difference to him
Completely free
   leaving it all to heaven
      he seems like a simpleton
No one catches
   a glimpse inside
      his mind
this old man
   all by himself
      between heaven and earth

Muso Soseki,
translated in the English
language by W. S. Merwin

28

31

41

A Woodcutter on His Way Home

Here and there little breezes stir the rushes.
At dusk the birds hurry as though they were lost.
Loaded with wood he moves slowly homeward.
He moves slowly, knowing the way.

Author unknown,
translated in the English language by W. S. Merwin,
in consultation with Nguyen Ngoc Bich

Pine Tree Tops

in the blue night
frost haze, the sky glows
with the moon
pine tree tops
bend snow-blue, fade
into sky, frost, starlight.
the creak of boots.
rabbit tracks, deer tracks,
what do we know.

Gary Snyder

١د

51

54

Joy Mountain

Grasses and trees
   look different
      and the auspices are good
Puffs of cloud
   delight in trailing
      around the peak
A thousand mountains
   a million hills
      look up to its virtue
Is there anyone
   who has never been blessed
      with its shelter

Muso Soseki,
translated in the English
language by W. S. Merwin

BHUTAN'S CURVE OF TIME

MARY PECK

Standing in the Present, on the highest point of the curve, you can look back and see the Past, or forward and see the Future, all in the same instant. Or, if you stand off to one side of the curve, as I am doing, your eye wanders from one to the other without any distinction.

M. WYLIE BLANCHET, *THE CURVE OF TIME*

In 1950 Tibet was invaded by China. Over the next ten years, many Tibetans fled to Nepal or India, and some escaped to Bhutan by making the climb over the Himalayan mountains. At that time Bhutan was a Buddhist monarchy, with barely half a million people, nearly every one of them a farmer. It was a country with a dynamic oral tradition and no written language, and with large expanses of unexplored and uninhabited land. No roads existed until the 1960s. The first tourists were allowed in limited numbers in 1974, and although more tourists are allowed today, the number is still controlled. Road construction is constant now, and television, the Internet, cell phones, and automobiles have arrived. As a young man, Bhutan's Fourth King had proposed the policy of Gross National Happiness to guide Bhutan's way forward. In 2001 he asked for the drafting of a constitution, which was presented in 2005, thus assuring the shift of government to a parliamentary democracy. He voluntarily abdicated and passed the throne to his twenty-six year old son in 2006.

My visits to the country between 1999 and 2005 were like standing on a curve of time—clearly able to see a way of life that had existed with very little change for generations, I could also see enormous change on the horizon. During my first week in Bhutan, a judge in Thimphu cautioned me not to harbor an idealistic view of the country or her people. While I have learned much about Bhutan since I left there (lessons from reading, very different from the lessons of walking) and about the big challenges that small countries face, what I saw in Bhutan was a landscape and culture that reminded me of Wallace Stegner's "personal expression of faith in the importance of geography, and especially wilderness, to human personality and culture."[1] Calling wilderness "the geography of hope," Stegner dreamed of a day when those in the American West would "create a society to match its scenery."[2] Bhutan was reassuring in its wholeness.

To cover long distances I traveled by car, but most of my photographs were made on treks that took me to villages and through parts of the country where roads did not yet exist. I was fortunate to have a visa that allowed me to travel to places usually off-limits to visitors, and to be a guest in Bhutanese homes in all parts of the country. Because most of Bhutan has never been mapped, I relied on Bhutanese guides, and they relied on the locals. Dechen and Pema guided me on my first trek through the Tang and Choskhor Valleys. Not trained as guides, they were nonetheless eager to accompany me because it gave these seventeen-year-old women from Bumthang an unusual opportunity to make an extended pilgrimage to the many small temples and sacred sites in those valleys—places that, although near to home, they had never been able to visit. We walked on animal paths when we could find them, and always asked directions along the way, which people gave us easily for their local areas. When we moved beyond the range of their instructions, we would ask again. Directions were never given in terms of distance or by estimating travel time, but always referred to the land or to landmarks—"over that range, cross just below the chorten in the curve of the crest." Once, in the Phobjika Valley, a man pointed in the direction we asked about and told us, "Just walk into that cloud."

For most Bhutanese, walking is still the primary means of transportation. On every trek we met people moving animals or supplies, or taking crops to trade or sell, and no one ever passed without stopping to talk. The conversations were so animated, spontaneous, and lengthy that it seemed these people knew each other intimately. Sometimes they did, but more often not; generosity of spirit, openness, and love of storytelling is simply the way throughout Bhutan. No one passed without an exchange, and when walking in the same direction, the conversations sometimes went on for miles.

At the school for traditional arts and crafts in the capital, Thimphu, students worked with a concentration that no disruption seemed to break. For long stretches they worked unsupervised at woodcarving, embroidery, sculpture, painting, and other traditional Buddhist arts. The stillness in these rooms filled with young people is a stillness found throughout the country. Away from the capital, in the villages, although a quiet moment was rare, the sounds of airplanes, traffic, television, telephones, and the range of machines and power tools in all their forms were absent. Instead the daily sounds were voices directing the movement of animals, animal bells, birdsong, flocks of snow pigeons taking flight, children singing, playing, and crying, water running, prayer wheels chiming, dogs barking, yak and sheep calling, wind rushing, people praying out loud, and the low tone of the conch shell—a ritual instrument—from the monastery at dawn and dusk.

A narrow one-lane road passes through Rafe, a village made up of one large extended family living in four houses. In 2003 Sonam, the matriarch of the clan, allowed me to stay with the family for several days. Guests usually sleep in the altar room, and I woke there each morning in the dark to Sonam's soft, low chanting as she made her morning offerings, followed by the sound of kestrels mating in the eaves of the small, immaculately tended family temple. The work of tending animals and crops went on around the clock; the family subsisted on what they were able to grow. The children were home for their two-month winter break from school, and were up before dawn doing chores. The man with the job of guarding the fields from wild boar went to work as everyone else went to bed. He kept watch on a bamboo platform overlooking the crops, and stood up to bang pans when he heard the animals approach. One evening everyone gathered in the altar room. The children swarmed around Sonam, and she tended to each one. She has been alive since the First King of Bhutan reigned, and like all Bhutanese, she expressed amazement at what the monarchs have done for the people of the country. The children sang in Dzongkha—some songs from memory, and others written. Fifteen months later I returned, and found this place—which had been so full of life—totally quiet. One of the young women who remained explained that her grandmother had gone to Thimphu to live with her daughter. Like many other villages in Bhutan, all but a caretaker had left for life in the capital city.

On a plateau above the Phobjika Valley is the village of Gante. Restoration of the four-hundred-year-old monastery in the village began in 2000, with the original buildings dismantled stone by stone. The soil that had made up the mortar was saved along with the old stones. Although some new stone was added, the mud mortar and plaster for the walls was mixed from the well-sifted original soil. The *zowpon* (head carpenter) worked without plans, a phone, or electrical power. Laborers talked and laughed as they worked, their voices accompanied by the sounds of handsaws and chisels, and of beams, ladders, and bamboo scaffolding being set in place. As in the original building, the 104 new wood pillars came from the local region, ornately carved and painted by hand by local craftsmen. The mural paintings were done in *dotshoen* (traditional mineral paints). Each community in the area sent carpenters and skilled workers, and *gomchens* (lay monks) from neighboring villages and settlements also provided labor. Seven statues of Buddha inside the temple were never touched—the restoration happened around them.

Spreading wide below this village, the broad wetland of the Phobjika Valley serves as a wintering site for the rare Black-necked (or Tibetan) Crane. In late October, the cranes begin arriving, congregating in groups throughout the valley. At the far western end of the valley is a small temple, Khewang, which holds its annual festival a few weeks before this. People arrive on foot and settle in the temple's open courtyard, which is surrounded by a very low rock wall; all are dwarfed by the expanse of wetland and sky. Young boys take turns on the drums as masked dancers fill the courtyard, changing their silk costumes throughout the day. A clown collects money for the temple, his bawdy jokes sparing no one. Bamboo baskets filled with *tso*, roasted rice laced with yak butter and sugar, are passed. The ritual dances end, and as the sun sets, people move in all directions for home, finally disappearing into every corner of the valley.

The ancient Buddhist and Bon practices that are still alive in Bhutan teach reverence for all life. More than one-quarter of Bhutan's territory, covering the full range of its major ecosystems, has been protected, and more than sixty percent of the native forest remains intact. Habitat for plants, birds, and other wildlife is extensive and tremendously varied, from the dense subtropical forest at an elevation of seven hundred feet along Bhutan's southern border with India, to the twenty-four-thousand-foot peaks of the Himalayas, well above tree line, where Bhutan meets the Tibetan plateau. Bhutan is the exception to the deforestation that has been the rule in the Himalayas, and broadleaf forest habitat, once widespread throughout the region at middle elevations, now thrives and survives only within Bhutan's borders. This forest is crucial to the country's rich biodiversity, and to the survival of the species that have retreated to this remaining habitat. Bhutan is home to some 600 bird species, at least 165 species of mammals, more than 800 orchids, over 50 species of rhododendrons, and more than 300 medicinal plants. Reports always qualify these numbers as approximate, as much of the country has never been surveyed. To get some idea of the concentration of diversity, consider that Bhutan is about half the size of Indiana, and that the entire United States has about 800 bird species. According to a study released by the Audubon Society and other organizations in March 2009, one-third of those species in the U.S. are endangered or threatened, primarily due to loss of habitat.[3]

Rebecca Pradhan, an ecologist and researcher for the Royal Society for the Protection of Nature, has been deeply involved in studying the broadleaf forest. Her work is not confined to the field; plant specimens fill her home, from the kitchen to the attic, and aspiring botanists whom she trains live in a small house on her property. At the monastery near her home, Pradhan organizes plantings, leading a hundred young monks who do the work; she also instructs the public about biodiversity and its importance, the impacts of human activities, and sustainable livelihoods. As Bhutan moves away from a culture of subsistence agriculture, work like Pradhan's is essential.

Bhutan's biological diversity exists because the human population has not overwhelmed it. The small, landlocked country is surrounded by India, Tibet, Myanmar/Burma, Nepal, Bangladesh, and Thailand. These neighboring countries with large populations (along with nearby China and Pakistan) can easily and dramatically affect Bhutan's ability to preserve her culture and traditions, as well as the wilderness that has been protected both through isolation and by intent. Increasing population everywhere poses these threats, but the potential impact and the costs are immediately apparent here.

In 2005, walking in the mountains above the village of Haa, I stepped off the narrow trail to allow a pack train to pass. We had heard it approaching for some time as we climbed the trail. A black-market pack train of seventy-nine horses—all loaded to capacity with carpets and enormous, bulging cardboard boxes with Chinese labels that swayed and scraped trees and brush as the horses worked their way downhill—passed on its way into Bhutan from occupied Tibet. The uphill trail from which they came was sprinkled with broken branches and bright plastic wrappers. Bhutan's border with Tibet could be reached within hours from that spot. In 1959, Bhutan and China agreed to honor the border between the Tibetan plateau and Bhutan as it existed at that time. Since then, Chinese soldiers have built roads into Bhutan along the northern border at six different places. Bhutan and China have been holding discussions about these roads since 1984, and in 2009 were planning their nineteenth round of meetings on the dispute.

What drew me to Bhutan were stories about a country of more wilderness than cultivated or developed land, with a government that considers protection of those lands important, and a culture with reverence for the land and its resources. After spending time in the country, I understand the cautionary comment of the judge in Thimphu: "We are human; we have the same troubles, the same problems." But I continue to see Bhutan as one "geography of hope." As the country opens itself to the world, those relentless pressures that wear on native cultures, wilderness, and humanity across the globe are at work. And while those forces build, Bhutan is further refining its policy of Gross National Happiness.

Epigraph. M. Wylie Blanchet, *The Curve of Time* (North Vancouver, Canada: Whitecap Books Ltd., 1968), p. 1.
1. Wallace Stegner, *The Sound of Mountain Water* (New York: Penguin Books, 1969), p. 11.
2. Stegner, pp. 38, 153.
3. *The State of the Birds, the 2009 Report*, http://www.stateofthebirds.org [last accessed November 19, 2009].

Notes by plate number

One of the great pleasures of traveling in Bhutan was the opportunity to talk with Bhutanese about their country. I recorded conversations with many people, and made notes of the more casual exchanges. On my return trips, I had photographs that allowed me to get more detailed explanations about what I had seen. Everyone was generous in taking time to talk about the country's landscape, beliefs, and customs. I am especially grateful to Rinpoche Mynak Tulku; Dasho Karma Ura, Centre for Bhutan Studies; Dago Tshering and Rebecca Pradhan, Royal Society for the Protection of Nature; Aum Chimela Wangmo and the nuns of Sisinang; and Dorji Phentso and Karma Sangay, Sakten Park Staff Foresters, for explaining with care—and patience—so much about Bhutan. These notes have been compiled from conversations and interviews with the many Bhutanese to whom I spoke; their varied voices are here. Any errors in understanding are mine.

1. *Tang Valley, Bumthang*

2. *Radi*

3. *Tashi Yangtse*

4. *Gante, Phobjika Valley*
A family in western Bhutan is drying chilies upstairs in the storage area of their home. Chilies are an essential ingredient in Bhutan's *ema datse*, a cheese sauce served with every meal. The home is made mostly of mud and wood, with corrugated iron for the roof. On the middle floor, where the family lives, is an open, mud-plastered hearth for cooking. Every dwelling has an altar room, which is used for daily offerings, various ceremonies throughout the year, and as a guest room. Not long ago, the family's animals would have lived beneath them in a basement area, but such an arrangement has become a thing of the past.

5. *Thri Dangbee, Kuri River Valley*
Bhutan is home to a type of red rice found nowhere else in the world; it is the nation's major agricultural crop. With rainfall and temperature varying widely among the country's many valleys, only the locally available foodstuffs have traditionally fed the Bhutanese people. But as life in Bhutan changes, this, too, is changing: Bhutan has begun exporting potatoes and importing rice and other packaged foods from India.

6. *Khotakha*
Kinley's home has had its annual blessing, signified by the pine bough on the roof. Every home hosts a lama (spiritual leader or guru) and a group of monks for this yearly ceremony, which takes place in December or January.

7. *Damji*
The boundaries between here and there are marked by bamboo fences, woven by hand. Like sandals, pack baskets, prayer flags, and herders' flutes, the fences serve their purpose and then return to the earth without a trace. The land is mapped only in the minds of locals.

8. *Threshing rice, Trongsa*

9. *Sonam, Jamby, Kencho, and Pema, schoolgirls in Ura*
Karma Ura, in Stan Armington's *Bhutan* (Lonely Planet Publications, 1998), writes of his native village of Ura:
"Despite astounding progress, some younger people expect more amenities to come in the next stage of development, and are anticipating an easier future. The older villagers think that enough has been provided, and now that everybody is comfortably above the hardship and the subsistence level, the next preoccupation of the village should be culture and faith. However, ambitious and materialistic youth think that the leaders live in the twilight of the past."

10. *Mongar*
Most Bhutanese travel by foot, sometimes trekking on mountain paths for days to reach distant destinations. But the lure of urban life is changing some traditional ways: the young have choices that their parents didn't have, and many are eager to leave their villages and move to the capital, Thimphu.

11. *Sangay feeding ants, Rangjung*
Sangay Dorji asked the local lama, "What offering can I make? I have nothing material to give." The lama replied, "Feed the ants." And so, every day, unless the ground is sodden, Sangay makes his way slowly, searching for anthills and stopping whenever he finds one to sprinkle his mixture of ground biscuit, wheat, and sugar.

12. Membartso, Bumthang

Prayer flags strung across rivers are a common sight. At Membartso, water races through the gorge, and the incessant wind sends out prayers from numerous strands of brightly colored cloth. The Bhutanese believe in protective deities—tree, stone, earth, and water gods among them. To respect these deities and leave them to themselves is a matter of grave importance. Disturbing them amounts to destroying their homes, and is believed to bring harm not only to those responsible, but also to the families or even the whole villages of the perpetrators. Rain will be lacking when most needed; hailstorms will destroy crops; disease or famine will claim many lives. All over Bhutan, people perform rituals to honor nature's deities, offering them thanks for the use of their resources.

13. Membartso, Bumthang

Simple and small, made easily from clay with an iron cast, *tsa tsas* are respected almost as highly as massive stupas (commemorative or reliquary mounds). To mold even a single *tsa tsa* is to earn great religious merit and generate auspicious circumstances for oneself and one's family. Each step in the making of a *tsa tsa* is an act of reverence. Kneading the clay, the creator recites mantras, imbuing the physical object with a spiritual essence. Grains of rice or paper prayer rolls, or even ashes from the dead, might be mixed into the clay. The offering is consecrated and dries in the sun. All over Bhutan, *tsa tsas* shelter in caves and crevices, stand in monasteries, or balance on rock walls.

14. Prayer flags, Taktsang

Water, earth, sunlight, air: the elements that provide for the making of prayer flags in due course reclaim them. Here, on the steep path to Taktsang Monastery, pilgrims and monks trek through lush pine forest, erecting shrines and cairns along the way to honor this most sacred site. Families make the climb with offerings and a picnic. The name Taktsang means Tiger's Nest, for it is said that on this spot in the seventh century, Guru Rinpoche (also known as Padmasambhava) arrived on a flying tigress and meditated for three months in a cave, quelling the demons that opposed the spread of Buddhism.

15. Gamri River

The nomadic people of Sakten in eastern Bhutan offer their dead to the Gamri River, as nourishment for fish and insects. It is a sacred ceremony. The nomads soak the body in water for several days, before removing and hiding the head, as it is difficult to look at a familiar face while cutting up the remains. Astrologers assign a relative the task of chopping the corpse into hundreds of pieces. Throughout these rituals, which will lead the deceased to the right path after death, the body is treated with respect. Along the water's edge, small flags fashioned of bamboo and handmade paper are placed as prayers.

16. Kyichu Temple, Paro

Kyichu Temple was one of the first two temples built when Buddhist teachings arrived in Bhutan in the seventh century. The faithful circumambulate the holy site in a steady flow, devoting themselves to the endless vow of awakening the compassionate heart. By reciting mantras of purification and turning prayer wheels set in the temple walls, they improve their own karma and spread goodwill and healing to others.

17. Trongsa Dzong

Dzongs in Bhutan—originally built as fortresses that housed both religion and government under one roof—continue to be used as government buildings and monasteries. Bhutan's monarchy began at this *dzong*, overlooking the Mangde River, and for centuries it was the religious and political center of Bhutan. In the fall, the monks walk to the Kurjey Monastery in Bumthang (where the climate is milder) and take up residence there for the winter.

18. Tashi, Trongsa festival

19. Trongsa festival

Bhutan's annual religious festivals, though sacred and solemn, are also convivial social events. The *thongdrol* (an oversized *thangka*, or banner) is unfurled on the last morning of the Trongsa festival. Bhutanese Buddhists believe that to view a *thongdrol* is to be spared from continued rebirths in the cycle of transmigration.

20. Tamshing Phala Choepa, Tamshing Monastery, Bumthang

Completed in 1505 (and in use ever since), Tamshing is now home to Bhutanese monks and a monastic community that came from Tibet seeking refuge in 1959. The dances they practice have been performed since the temple's founding. The annual Tamshing Phala Choepa goes on for three days. The masked dancers continue through heat, hail, and heavy rain. Pine branches burning in ceremonial ovens fill the courtyard with their scent and smoke.

21. Gante
In 2003, the King of Bhutan led the army to southern Bhutan and to war. For more than twelve years, armed groups that had crossed from India had been living in the dense jungles of southern Bhutan and returning to India to fight, hoping to advance the cause of a separate state for Assam and West Bengal. The area had been off-limits to any visitors for years, and was becoming increasingly dangerous. The King's requests that the camps be abandoned and that the separatists leave Bhutan were ignored, and the raids continued. In January 2004, this rarely practiced ceremony to protect troops in battle was performed at Gante.

22. Tamshing Phala Choepa,
Tamshing Monastery, Bumthang
On the final day of the ceremony, lamas enter the courtyard wearing masks that have been used for generations. Between dances, people rush to line up for blessings from the masked figures. Many people prostrate themselves in the courtyard to express reverence and respect.

23. Gingser Puja, Merak
Arriving in the courtyard of the temple, villagers bow, place their offerings on a stone wall that also serves as the altar, and sit behind the monks.

Like food everywhere in Bhutan, the offerings—baskets of rice, cheese wrapped in rhododendron leaves, and *doma* (chewing quids made from crushed areca nut with lime rolled up in a betel leaf)—are plentiful, consist mostly of rice, and are made from what is grown locally. Over the course of the morning a large group gathers. A blackened pot, steaming with warm *ara* (a mild alcoholic beverage), cooks behind the crowd.

24. Dechen Phodrang Monastery, Thimphu
Even today, monks receive some of the best education that Bhutan has to offer. As boys, they learn to read, write, and recite and memorize prayers. At fifteen or sixteen, they begin to specialize: the best thinkers study philosophy, eventually graduating from one of the monastic colleges and earning the title of *geshe*, or spiritual friend; the boys gifted in mathematics are generally encouraged to study astrology; and those with artistic talent develop their creative skills, focusing especially on mandala design. To qualify as a *pandit*, or great scholar, a monk must be adept in all five of the minor sciences (poetry, semantics, lexicography, astrology, and dance and drama), as well as the five major sciences (grammar, medicine, painting and handicraft, logic, and philosophy).

25. Learning to read,
Dechen Phodrang Monastery, Thimphu
In the beginning, use a stick to point to each letter, and recite it. Be diligent. Memorize the sutras, and understand the commentaries that accompany them. If you do well on the examination, your teacher will praise you: "*Lagso*"—"Well done."

26. Calligraphy practice,
Dechen Phodrang Monastery, Thimphu
First, dry bamboo in smoke. Next, cut small pieces and carve them into pens. Let each pen have the pliancy to sweep wide, and also to trace a fine edge. Take care. Practice on a blackboard first—you can clean the board with ash and start over. After a year, move on to paper, giving each letter your full attention. If you become a master, you might one day be copying the sutras in gold and silver.

27. Sonam studying sutras, Shechen Orgyen
Chozong Nunnery, Sisinang, Paro
In the 1960s, fire destroyed the temple at Sisinang, and the local community offered the site to H.H. Dilgo Khyentse Rinpoche. Under the guidance of this revered sage, the temple was rebuilt, and a nunnery established. Dilgo Khyentse's wife, Sangyum Lhamo, took charge, and the nunnery grew. The women there today come from extremely poor families or families with difficulties; some are orphans or school dropouts. As long as there is room, anyone who applies receives a place. The day begins with *puja*, or prayer, and continues with a period of cleaning, followed by classroom study. Lessons consist of reading and writing, memorizing prayers, and learning to play religious instruments and make offerings. Nuns suited to further study learn Buddhist philosophy.

28. Making butter lamps, Shechen Orgyen Chozong Nunnery, Sisinang, Paro
The lamps, which always remain lit, burn yak butter or vegetable oil. The temple is open to visitors, and anyone may stay there on retreat.

29. Dugna Primary School
In this remote mountain region, even the youngest students board through the school year in one large house near their schoolrooms—in all, thirty boys in two rooms on the ground floor, and twenty-five girls upstairs. Their days begin and end with prayers. Twice a year, for two weeks in summer and two months in winter, they walk home to their parents, a trip that may take a full day.

30. Bomdeling Community School
Daily News Board: *Our national flag is a symbol. When we look at it, we think of our country, Bhutan.* Students learn their lessons in English, and study the national tongue, Dzongkha, as a subject. Dzongkha is also spoken in local dialects. Less than fifty years ago, Bhutan had eleven schools; today, there are nearly five hundred. Children must attend, but until quite recently, rural families often pleaded to keep their sons and daughters at home to care for animals and work the land.

31. Kuzendrug Monastery, Tang Valley, Bumthang

32. Tharpaling Monastery, Bumthang
The ritual of *lhasang*—purification with smoke—takes place each day, and especially on the fifteenth day of the fifth month of the annual almanac. On that holy day, called *dzamling kyisang*, people in many parts of the Himalayas make smoke offerings to the mountain deities, burning sandalwood, juniper, or other sacred woods, and planting "wind horse" prayer flags to honor the land and ask for the health and protection of its life-giving resources. Here Buddhism and conservation make good partners, sharing a concern for the environment and a commitment to responsible use of its bounty.

33. Restoration, Gante Monastery
As part of the restoration of the four-hundred-year-old monastery, craftsman from nearby villages apply *dotshoen* (mineral paints) ground from local soils, the most aesthetic and durable of the traditional pigments, to the mural paintings on the *lhakhang* (temple).

34. Kezang, Gante
One of the many questions Bhutan faces is what type of work the new generation of educated youth will do. Most of them know little about farming, and the life of a village farmer does not appeal to them. Kezang has been trained as a woodcarver, and is performing intricate restoration work on the lintels of Gante Monastery. Like many Bhutanese young people, he dreams of finding a way to come to the United States, imagining that he would continue his woodcarving work there.

35. Tamshing Monastery, Bumthang

36. Lama Lopen Pemala, Nyimalung
Lama Lopen Pemala was born in Bumthang in 1926. While *lama* means "religious master," *lopen* is a term of further respect for the most learned of monks. Pemala was an author, iconographer, astronomer/astrologer, historian, architect, tailor, and many other things. His monastic training began when he was eight years old. He soon became the pupil of Doring Tulku, a revered and demanding teacher from Tibet who taught at Nyimalung Monastery. When the boy was fifteen, the lama returned to Tibet, and three years later Pemala traveled secretly across the border—making the perilous mountain journey on foot—to continue studying with his master. After two years, Doring sent Pemala back to Bhutan, where the young man became one of Bhutan's most important teachers and scholars, writing the first definitive history of his country and the first book on the grammar, phonetics, and spelling of the Dzongkha language. Until his death in 2009, Lopen Pemala lived in the Bumthang Valley as chief abbot of Nyimalung Monastery, which he had watched being built as a boy.

37. Tashi Dorji, Kuzendrug
Among the many public duties of a young monk is "reading the dice," a form of fortune-telling that the Bhutanese take seriously and rely upon when making decisions. Interpreting the dice is a bit like consulting the *Tao Te Ching*.

38. Shepherds, Phobjika Valley

39. Feeding yak, Merak

40. Sakten
In the village of Sakten, far from even the most primitive roads, nomadic yak herders take shelter and regroup. Untouched by modern life—Sakten has no televisions, cars, telephones, or power tools—this is nonetheless a noisy place: as babies cry and children play, herders direct their yak and sheep, belled animals bleat and grunt, birdsong peppers the air, the whir of snow pigeons taking wing mingles with the rush of wind and water, and men and women pray out loud. From the monastery, the conch shell calls before dawn and at dusk. At the edge of the village, on their way to begin the climb up Nachung Pass, this mother and daughter wear a typical mix of traditional and contemporary clothing. Saktenpas wear yak-hair vests and red felt jackets (seen on every Sakten schoolchild) made from yak wool. Mother and daughter will spin wool while they watch the yaks on the pass, where rhododendron may grow to a height of thirty feet. As they climb the pass, they will not smell the many flowers in bloom, due to a belief that this will cause altitude sickness.

41. Goat herder, Chukka
This young goat herder in Chukka is descended from Nepalese who settled in Bhutan generations ago. Scores of thousands of Nepalese settlers lived in other areas of southern Bhutan for generations. In 1990, Bhutan expelled more than one hundred thousand of them, despite the fact that many were born in Bhutan and some owned businesses and homes there. Since their expulsion, most have been confined to camps in Nepal, where their status as stateless refugees prohibits them from working, traveling, or putting down roots. In October 2006, the United States stepped in, offering to resettle sixty thousand of them in the coming years. Bhutan prepared a Human Rights Report in preparation for a United Nations Human Rights Review in Geneva in December 2009 that addressed the ongoing refugee situation (among other things). Bhutan is committed to finding a solution to this problem, which the government considers an issue of illegal immigration and a continuing security threat.

42. Dugna

43. Samtengang
Efforts are underway to reduce the amount of wood gathered and to educate people on ways to cut wood without depleting forested areas, but families still depend on firewood for cooking and warmth. The daily trip to gather this essential fuel is often a task for the elderly.

44. Chicken coop, Chukka

45. Making yeast for ara or chang, Gomphu
The mild alcoholic beverages *ara* and *chang* are commonly consumed in eastern Bhutan. Alcohol has featured in Bhutanese culture for hundreds of years, in both religious rites and social celebrations. As *duetsi* (one of the five precious elements), it is offered to the gods in a human skull cup; as *marchang*, it is imbibed to invoke blessings on new ventures. It is served to welcome guests, to bid them farewell, to celebrate marriages, to treat the sick, and to soothe new mothers after childbirth. It is even served during archery competitions, to enhance the confidence of players by releasing inhibitions. Today, however, heavy consumption of alcohol is widespread in Bhutan—and related problems are increasing. The government has responded, restricting hours for licensed bars and banning consumption of homemade brews in public places. *Om mani padme hum*, the mantra of Avalokiteshvara, the Bodhisattva of Compassion, is painted on rock walls in every region; sometimes, alongside it, is a warning about the harmful effects of alcohol abuse.

46. Black-faced Langour, Royal Manas National Park

47. Blue Pine

48. Hermitage, Taktsang, Paro

49. Prayer wall, Gasa
Mani (prayer) walls, *chortens* (shrines), and prayer flags appear on every horizon in Bhutan. They are present in river valleys and on mountain peaks, by roads and near religious sites, in populated places and far from human habitation. People build them to earn spiritual merit, or sometimes to bless the site where a death occurred. On the walls, a prayer—often *om mani padme hum*, the mantra of Avalokiteshvara—is carved into a row of stones all the way around. Walkers passing a *mani* wall always circumambulate it in prayer.

50. Merak River, Mindula Pass

A heap of stones speaks of where a chorten once stood. The chorten is based on the Indian stupa, a commemorative or reliquary mound that represents the enlightened mind of the Buddha. Today shrines in Bhutan are dismantled and robbed of their relics with increasing frequency. Such desecration carries a heavy penalty for those who are caught.

51. Phobjika Valley

Among the mountains of east Wangdue lies the quiet valley of Phobjika. Here, in its sheltered wetlands, Black-necked Cranes, migrants from the arid plains of Tibet in the north, pass the winter months. The endangered birds—distinguished by their red crowns, black tails, and ash-gray bodies—are sacred in Bhutan. Safe from persecution, they often feed near human settlements, as they depend on grazing cattle to expose the roots of the dwarf bamboo that covers the valley floor.

52. Black-necked Cranes, Phobjika Valley

The Black-necked (or Tibetan) Crane breeds on the Qinghai-Tibetan plateau in China and (to a lesser degree) in adjacent Ladakh in India. Along with sites in India and China, the Phobjika Valley is one of several lower-elevation wintering grounds. The main threats facing the species—famous for its breathtaking dance displays and coordinated mating calls—are the loss and degradation of its habitat (especially winter wetlands) through irrigation, drainage, and other human activities. Bhutan's Royal Society for the Protection of Nature has established an education and study center in the valley.

53. Mangde River, Shemgang

With more than sixty percent of its original forest cover intact, Bhutan is facing myriad questions about development and conservation. Some people advocate rapid development of housing and infrastructure, especially the construction of extensive road systems, increased mining activity, and more logging. Others plead for the protection of the forests and habitat that have made Bhutan's biodiversity unique.

54. Sakten

Small mounds of prayer flags and offerings surround the base of these ancient trees. The temple they conceal is no longer used or maintained, but the trees are venerated, and people come here often to offer prayers.

55. Chukka

56. Kuri River, Thrumshingla National Park

The ancient Buddhist and Bon practices that are still alive in Bhutan teach reverence for all life. They are reflected in the work of villagers who, as part of a community forest system, make decisions on local land use; and in the government's protection of more than one-quarter of Bhutan's territory, covering the full range of its major ecosystems. Four national parks have been established. In a few places, long-enduring villages exist within the parks, and some of the land is used for agriculture and pasture. At this juncture in Bhutan's history, allowing such villages to remain while protecting large tracts of undeveloped land is part of the government's attempt to establish material wellbeing without destroying the country's indigenous culture or rich biological diversity.

RELATED WEBSITES

The Centre for Bhutan Studies, http://www.bhutanstudies.org.bt/?page_id=2 [last accessed August 22, 2011].

International Crane Foundation, Black-necked Crane page, http://www.savingcranes.org/blackneckedcrane.html [last accessed July 29, 2011].

Kuensel Online, Bhutan's daily news site (website of Bhutan's English-language newspaper), http://www.kuenselonline.com/ [last accessed July 29, 2011].

Royal Society for Protection of Nature, http://www.rspnbhutan.org/ [last accessed July 29, 2011].

Suggested Reading

As a small landlocked country, Bhutan is greatly affected by what goes on in the surrounding region. The following books—the majority of them not specifically about Bhutan—helped my understanding of the big problems that small countries face. India's need for hydropower, and the history and struggles of Tibet and Sikkim are relevant for Bhutan, as are issues of wildlife conservation and environmental protection.

Baker, Ian. *The Heart of the World: A Journey to the Last Secret Place*.
New York: Penguin Press, 2004.
   Baker's descriptions of his travels in search of the legendary Tsangpo Gorge in Tibet relate in great detail the satisfactions and difficulties of traveling in uncharted Himalayan territory, and provide insight into the experience of trekking in parts of Bhutan.

Datta-Ray, Sunanda K. *Smash and Grab: Annexation of Sikkim*. New Delhi: Vikas Publishing House, 1984.
Rustomji, Nari. *Sikkim: A Himalayan Tragedy*. New Delhi: Allied Publishers Private Limited, 1987.
   No longer shown on maps is Sikkim, which sits between Bhutan and Nepal. The Buddhist monarchy of Sikkim became a protectorate of India in 1950, and ceased to exist as an independent nation when it was absorbed by India in 1975, becoming the twenty-second Indian state. Nepalese had been migrating to Sikkim and Bhutan for many years, and in 1975 made up three-quarters of Sikkim's population of 210 thousand. Maps of India from this era show both Sikkim and Bhutan as part of India. These books by Datta-Ray and Rustomji explain the time of transition in Sikkim, and provide important context for Bhutan's fears about unregulated immigration.

Desai, Kiran. *The Inheritance of Loss*. New York: Atlantic Monthly Press, 2006.
   The characters in this novel live on the Indian side of the Himalayas, land that—in this area of historically fluid borders—once belonged to Bhutan. The multitude of issues that they face, including globalization, emigration and immigration, terrorism, and the lure of the West, are common to Bhutan and her neighbors. While many books about life in the Himalayas portray these places as Shangri-la, Desai examines the underside of that ideal: "The country had seemed unreal—so full of fairy tales, of travelers seeking Shangri-la—it had proved all the easier to destroy, therefore" (p. 128).

Fletcher, Harold R. *A Quest of Flowers: The Plant Explorations of Frank Ludlow and George Sherriff Told from Their Diaries and Other Occasional Writings*.
Edinburgh: Edinburgh University Press, 1975; reprint, 1976.
   Ludlow and Sherriff made six expeditions to Bhutan and Tibet between 1933 and 1949. In Bhutan, they traveled with assistance and a full staff provided by the royal family. The book recounts their botanical and wildlife collecting activities, and includes great detail about the landscape and people they encountered. Preceding Ian Baker in his search for the Tsangpo Gorge, Ludlow and Sherriff were never successful; their last planned trip in 1949 was cancelled when the Chinese Army "reached Sining and had announced that in due course it would proceed to 'liberate' Tibet" (p. 351).

Hilton, Isabel. *The Search for the Panchen Lama*. New York: W.W. Norton & Company, 2000.
   The Panchen Lama is a revered religious figure for Tibetans, second only to the Dalai Lama. In 1995, Tibetan religious leaders selected a young boy to succeed the tenth Panchen Lama (who had died in 1989). The boy disappeared almost immediately—reportedly taken into custody by Chinese authorities—and has not been seen since. The book recounts the incident, the role of the Chinese, and Tibetan religious infighting and politics, and reveals the Chinese effort to control the selection of a most important religious figure as an attempt to even further control Tibet and her religious autonomy.

Hilton, James. *Lost Horizon*. New York: Simon & Schuster, Inc., 1960.
   Originally published in 1936, the novel explores life in Shangri-la, a hidden monastery in Tibet that intended to remain isolated from the world.

Matthiessen, Peter. *The Birds of Heaven: Travels with Cranes*. Paintings and drawings by Robert Bateman. New York: North Point Press, 2001.

Describing his worldwide journey to find cranes in their various habitats, Peter Matthiessen devotes a full chapter to his travels in Bhutan to the wintering grounds of the Black-necked or Tibetan Crane, revered there as *trung trung*. Like all wildlife, the Black-necked Crane acknowledges no national boundaries, and its territory includes Bhutan, India, the Tibetan plateau, and China. Through his travels, Matthiessen also erases boundaries and reminds us that, "These elegant birds, in their stature, grace, and beauty, their wild fierce temperament, are striking metaphors for the vanishing wilderness of our once bountiful earth" (p. xiv).

Mishra, Pankaj. *Temptations of the West: How to Be Modern in India, Pakistan, Tibet, and Beyond*. New York: Farrar, Straus and Giroux, 2006.

Writing not about Bhutan, but about her neighbors (India, Pakistan, Nepal, Afghanistan, and Tibet), Mishra examines contemporary changes in those countries. As Mishra lives and moves between Britain and India, he suggests that many countries in Asia, having been under the spell of Western values, would now like to define modernization on their own terms. In light of the influence that the West has already had, he holds out the most hope for Tibet: "faced with an aggressively secular materialism, they may still prove, almost alone in the world, how religion … can be a source of cultural identity and moral values; how it can become a means of political protest without blinding the devout with hatred and prejudice" (p. 322).

Norberg-Hodge, Helena. *Ancient Futures: Learning from Ladakh*. San Francisco: Sierra Club Books, 2009.

Ricard, Matthieu. *Journey to Enlightenment: The Life and World of Khyentse Rinpoche, Spiritual Teacher from Tibet*. New York: Aperture, 1996.

The Dalai Lama begins his Remembrance in this book with the words, "Dilgo Khyentse Rinpoche is one of my most revered teachers" (p. 7). Khyentse was a teacher to many, including Ricard, the author and photographer of this book, who was his student and personal assistant for the last fourteen years of the master's life. Ricard traveled with Khyentse in Nepal, Bhutan, and India, and accompanied him when the teacher was finally able to return to Tibet. Khyentse, who had escaped from Tibet with his family, was invited to rebuild the old Sisinang Temple near Paro after it burned down in the 1960s. Along with his wife, Sangyum (Khandro Lhamo), Khyentse took charge of the rebuilt temple and established a nunnery, which continues to thrive today.

Rustomji, Nari. *Enchanted Frontiers: Sikkim, Bhutan and India's North-eastern Borderlands*. Calcutta: Oxford University Press, 1973.

A very personal account of the author's journeys, on foot, from Sikkim to Bhutan, and his visits with the Bhutanese royal family in the 1950s, during the reign of the Third King. The book provides a look at Bhutan before it was opened to the world, when serfdom was still the rule, and gives an interesting and supportive perspective on Bhutan's long policy of isolation.

Schicklgruber, Christian, and Françoise Pommaret, eds. *Bhutan: Mountain Fortress of the Gods*. London: Serindia Publications, 1997.

With essays by nine scholars, this extensively illustrated academic book details in depth the customs and traditions, crafts, and religious rituals of Bhutan, along with the origins of the country's ethnic diversity.

Tabuchi, Satoru. *Festival and Faith at Nyimalung*. With contributions by Mynak Tulku, Karma Ura, and Yoshiro Imaeda. Tokyo: Hirakawa Shuppan Inc., 2002.

A detailed photographic documentation of monastic life and the ritual celebrations at Nyimalung Monastery in the Bumthang Valley. Beginning with a description of the history of Bhutan and the country's Buddhist roots, the text gives an intimate description of life at Nyimalung and in the surrounding valley, with a look at the devotional life of a valley apple farmer, the daily life of a monk, the liturgy and iconography at Nyimalung, and the creation of the monastery's *thongdrol* (oversized *thangka*, or banner).

ACKNOWLEDGMENTS

The former U.N. Ambassador from Bhutan, Lyonpo Om Pradhan, and Dr. Marshall Bouton assisted in arranging a visa, making my first visit to Bhutan possible. Dr. Mark Mancall was generous with his knowledge of the country, and provided introductions that helped me during my travels there.

Robert and Kerstin Adams and Edward Ranney took time to look at the editing and sequencing of the photographs. Kate Watson unraveled pages of notes and interviews to develop the first draft of the notes on the photographs, and Laurie Senauke took great care in undertaking the initial editing of Dr. Karma Ura's interview. Melanie B.D. Klein brought her knowledge of Buddhism and her skill as a manuscript editor to those drafts, and Catherine Mills, with great patience, extended herself far beyond the work of designing the book. James Ballinger's early and continued commitment to exhibit the photographs at the Phoenix Art Museum played an important role in the publication of the book.

A project such as this that spans many years and involves unusual travel and publication expenses was possible only because a handful of friends, with an understanding of Bhutan's uniqueness, provided funds to begin and finish this work.

The generosity of the Bhutanese people shaped how I saw their country, and when I returned home a similar generosity was offered by Ruth Pickering and Linda Lasure, Dessa Bokides and Will Fay, Lynn Moser, and Jerry Richardson. Like the Bhutanese, they opened their homes, shared their families, and provided me with a place to work.

MERLIN PRESS LLC   PHOENIX ART MUSEUM
© 2011 MARY PECK. ALL RIGHTS RESERVED. ISBN 978-0-615-49933-8

"Pine Tree Tops" by Gary Snyder, from *Turtle Island*, copyright © 1974 by Gary Snyder. Reprinted by permission of New Directions Publishing Corp.

"Old Man at Leisure" by Muso Soseki, translated in the English language by W.S. Merwin, currently collected in *East Window: The Asian Translations*. Translation copyright © 1998 by W.S. Merwin, used with permission of The Wylie Agency LLC. All rights reserved.

"Joy Mountain" by Muso Soseki, translated in the English language by W.S. Merwin, currently collected in *East Window: The Asian Translations*. Translation copyright © 1998 by W.S. Merwin, used with permission of The Wylie Agency LLC. All rights reserved.

"A Woodcutter on His Way Home," author unknown, translated in the English language by W.S. Merwin, in consultation with Nguyen Ngoc Bich, currently collected in *East Window: The Asian Translations*. Translation copyright © 1998 by W.S. Merwin, used with permission of The Wylie Agency LLC. All rights reserved.

Dr. Ura's essay, "Tradition and Culture in Bhutan," was compiled and edited from interviews with Dr. Karma Ura conducted in 1999 and 2000 by Mary Peck, and in 2008 by the Bhutan Broadcasting Service.

The Manuscript Editor for this book was Melanie B.D. Klein. The book was designed by Catherine Mills Design, Seattle, and the typeface is New Clear Era by Bob Aufuldish/Fontboy. The duotone negatives were made by Thomas Palmer, Newport, Rhode Island. The books were printed by Meridian Printing, East Greenwich, Rhode Island, under the supervision of Danny Frank, and bound by Roswell Bookbinding, Phoenix.

No part of this book may be reproduced or transmitted in any form or by any means, electronic or mechanical, including photocopying and recording, or in any information storage or retrieval system without the prior written permission of Merlin Press LLC.

Library of Congress Cataloging-in-Publication Data
Peck, Mary, 1952–
   Bhutan : between heaven and earth / photographs by Mary Peck ;
   essay by Karma Ura
   p. cm.
Includes bibliographical references.
ISBN 978-0-615-49933-8
1. Bhutan—Pictorial works. I. Karma Ura, 1961– II. Title.
DS491.42.P44 2011
954.98—dc23   2011025948